FINDING PURPOSE AND JOY…
It's a Journey

By

Roger Laidig

D1127853

Copyright 2014 Roger Laidig

Print Edition
 ISBN: 978-1-312-12744-9

All rights are owned by the author and written permission from the author is needed for any copying, storage and retrieval, digital or printed, by any other person. Infringement of this can and will result in legal action.

Acknowledgments

My inspiration for writing this book came from several different places. The truth is that a lot of it came from just living life, having some successes, and having even more failures. Actually, in hindsight, they weren't failures since my greatest times of learning have happened when things didn't go the way I thought they should and were very painful. Interestingly I believe that I am learning more in the years after I turned 60 than before. Why? Because I no longer have a need to be right and prove my worth. My motto now has become "hang on loosely". What that means to me is to diligently try my best to make good decisions, do what is right, and desire, not demand, the best outcome. Since there is so much that is out of my control, I am learning to trust the sovereignty of God of our Universe to handle the details.

That said, my greatest lessons have started at home with my wonderful wife, Susan, and our two now married sons, Ryan and Joel. Through the years, they were able to help me see my shortcomings (blind spots) because we were virtually together continually. Although I didn't necessarily welcome their 'constructive' insight on my ways, retrospectively I am realizing how much I am blessed to have them in my life. So I am dedicating this book to you, Susan, Ryan, and Joel and your families. So Crystal, Kamryn, and Landyn and Kendra, Mikayli, and Silas, you too are a huge part of making me to believe that I am the most blessed man in the world.

In addition, much of my learning has come from my larger family and friends, my days of being part of the work family at Laidig, Inc. for 30 years. While I'm tempted to mention names as some were more influential than others, I don't want to take the chance of unintentionally excluding anyone. Other sources of influence came from the church, through seminars, and through the writings of several brilliant authors including Gary Smalley, Charles Swindoll, Stephen Covey and his sons, Richard Carlson, Richard Rohr, Ken Blanchard, Spencer Johnson, John Maxwell, and Todd Gongwer. You will probably recognize many insights from their writings. It not only takes a village to raise a child, it also a community to help each person successfully navigate the journey called life.

From the technical side of actually writing a book, author Garrett Pierson's free video series and book, "How to Write a Book ASAP" served as my guide. Elizabeth Hayes of Nova Scotia, who I found through Elance.com, skillfully provided the services of cover design, proofreading, the steps of publishing, and releasing this book. What a great help they were. I am very grateful for their guidance and services.

In the big picture, my greatest inspiration is coming from the Word and instruction of the Greatest Teacher that has walked this Earth. It is my hope and desire to continually grow in His attitude and attributes. The Bible verses referenced are from the New International Version (NIV) with the exception of a few minor changes that were based on the way I memorized them in the past.

Table of Contents

Finding Purpose and Joy is a Journey?

Warning: If you're hoping for a 'Get Rich and Famous' book, this book is not for you.

A HEART ATTACK! Me? No way. I'm only 52 years old and in decent health! Heart attacks happen to others but surely not me. That's what I was thinking on April 30, 1999, about an hour after I asked my oldest sister, Nita, how I could get rid of the acid reflux that I had been experiencing. Nita had an extensive background in nursing so she was a logical person to ask. In return, she asked me a series of questions. Shortly thereafter she was insistent that we head directly to the hospital. Sure enough, it was a heart attack. After 3 stents were well placed in blood vessels that were 95 to 99% blocked, I started my way to recovery. I am very thankful for this outcome as it doesn't always turn out this way.

As strange as it may seem, retrospectively, that event was one of the best things that ever happened to me. In fact, there is a good chance that I may not have written this book without that life-changing event. After I became stabilized, I asked my doctor what I could do to live a reasonably healthy life in the future. He told me 3 things:
1. Eat right
2. Exercise regularly
3. Learn to manage stress

The first two things were pretty easy if a person was committed to it and I was. I soon learned that the third one, 'Learn to manage stress', was not so easy but it did lead me to become open to things that I hadn't considered very much in the past. No longer would I take life and health for granted. It was time to begin contemplating, why am I on this Earth? What is my purpose? And how can I live it with joy in a way that might bring joy to others as well? I didn't realize it at the time, but I suppose that is the event that actually prompted me to unwittingly start writing this book. So here we go.

Which question would you likely answer 'yes' to? Do we think ourselves into a new way of living? Or, do we live ourselves into a new way of thinking? And why is this important to consider?

It is true that we generally can learn things like the "**3 R**'s" – Reading, 'Riting, and 'Rithmetic" by thinking and studying books. But can the same be said when it comes to the heart, mind, soul, and life in general?

After I graduated from college and post graduate work, I was relatively sure that while I needed to learn a lot more about maturity, having experienced all aspects of college life to the extreme, I had a lot of things about life figured out. After all, I had received my engineering degree from Purdue and shortly thereafter earned my graduate degree from Indiana University in South Bend. It was really pretty simple. If you thought like I thought, you were right. And if you didn't, you were wrong.

Now, after 6 decades on this earth, my view on being 'right' about most everything, has greatly diminished. In fact, in all sincerity, the older I get, the more I realize that I have so much more yet to learn. So the question is, "How did I go from 'knowing it all' to a place that I have only scraped the tip of the iceberg about what there is yet to learn?" And the exciting thing is that it has led me to a place where life seems to be bringing me more purpose and joy than I have ever experienced before.

What I have come to realize is that, at least for me, finding purpose and joy is a journey. And no point along the way was or is a destination.

So the reason that I decided to embark on writing this book is that several people have urged me to consider writing one. Until now, I have not felt peace that I was ready to do so. What has opened me up to doing it now is that perhaps some of the steps of the journey that I have taken along the way may be able to somehow help you find more purpose and joy earlier in life than I did. As I write this, I want you to know that my hope is merely that you will consider these steps and then make your own decisions about what is relevant to you. And I hope you will realize that these steps are not inspired or perfect. While I do believe that they are based on the principles that are generally true for all mankind, we all have different temperaments and circumstances in life that affect how we see and process things.

One of the greatest lessons that I have learned and still am reminded of is that a person generally will resist learning new ways of thinking on issues of their heart, soul, and mind until they are ready to learn. And they aren't ready to learn until they see a need to learn. And the need to learn doesn't come until they have experienced enough **pain** that they become open to realizing that it would be good, if not necessary, to re-evaluate and perhaps change in some ways.

So that brings us full circle to the original questions of this introduction... "Do we think ourselves into a new way of living?" Or, "Do we live ourselves into a new way of thinking?" For me, I can with certainty say that I have needed to learn to become open to new ways of thinking through living, running into some walls, and bloodying my nose.

So where are you at? Are you happy with the way your life is flowing? If you are, this book may have little meaning to you at this stage of your life. On the other hand, if you're finding yourself in the 'rat race' of life and perhaps you're starting to question, "Is this really what life is all about? Is this all there is?", maybe you'll be open to at least considering that there just might still be hope for something fresh for your remaining days here on Earth.

Either way, wherever you find yourself today, remember, this is not the destination. Rather, it's merely one point in time on your journey. It is the first day of the rest of your life. Your yesterdays are simply history for you to learn from and it's good to reflect on them. But for better or worse, please don't stay there. Your history is a gift to consider what you can learn from it. What parts brought you joy and what parts brought you pain? While it's not possible to change the past, you most certainly can influence greatly what your future is going to be.

So my hope is that you will look forward to your future with lots of hope that you too may find more purpose and joy in your lives.

POINTS TO PONDER
- Do we think ourselves into a new way of living? Or, do we live ourselves into a new way of thinking? And why is this important to consider?
- Why is it important to realize that we are on a journey and no place is the destination?
- Where are you at today? Are you content? Anxious? In the rat race?
- Do you desire to 'grow' past where you currently are?

The First Half of My Journey

I have shared parts of my journey in the chapter before. If you are interested, here is the rest of the story.

I was raised on a farm in northern Indiana in a fine Christian home. Since my Dad and Mom had come through the depression, the driving force was survival grounded in hard work. Mom was one of the nicest and kindest people that I have ever known. In addition to raising us 6 children, she fixed 3 solid meals every day, managed a good sized garden, washed clothes, helped each of us children, and was above reproach at treating each of us equally down to the very same number and value of gifts at Christmas. Looking back, I don't know how she did it. Dad was a man of high character and very few words. When he spoke, it was worthwhile to listen. The tone that he set around the farm was get up, milk the cows, eat breakfast, go back out and do the work of a grain and milk cow farm, come in for dinner (now we would say lunch), go back out and work hard doing the farm work, milk the cows, come eat supper, and go to bed. We went to church faithfully on Sunday mornings and Wednesday nights. Sundays were generally a day of rest except for milking the cows morning and night. Sundays were also a time for visiting with church friends. Our games included 'Andy-I-Over' and 'Who's Afraid of the Big Bad Wolf?'. We lived by modest means as all the profits were re-invested in the land. It was a good life in its own way.

Dad hated debt. He taught me a few simple lessons about money. 1. Always make sure you have more money going into the moneybox than you take out. 2. Never borrow money on anything that doesn't increase in value. 3. Find a way to make money while you're sleeping. It was simple but wise advice.

The church that we attended was Biblically fundamental and filled with solid salt-of-the-earth people. That was fine for me when I was a child. As I grew older and went to college, I no longer connected with that form of worship. I wasn't against it but when I was exposed to the wide world that college exposed me to, I joined in on those festivities. And while I did learn some things from books, I also learned a whole lot more about the world. It was fun but I could sense that it also was leading me down the wrong path. Toward the end of college and at the beginning of my real work world, I felt a void in my life. I really did want to follow Christ and exhibit the character that my parents had taught me but I wasn't able to do it. I tried in my own strength to live a lifestyle that would make my family and God proud, but failed miserably.

When I was 23, I met my future wife, Susan. As I began realizing that we would be getting married, I found myself wanting to become more mature and responsible. She didn't come from the same church background that I did so when I would tell her that I wanted to follow Jesus and be 'saved', she had no idea what I was talking about. And when we tried to talk about it, we both got frustrated so we just avoided the conversation and were 'Chreasters'. This means that we went to church on Christmas and Easter.

Then when Susan was pregnant with our 2nd son, the doctors detected a disease in her body but chose not to do testing until Joel was born. After several failed attempts, they were finally able to retrieve the necessary material from her kidneys. This tissue was then sent to Chicago where they blew the images up on large screens. And then came the bomb. Our nephrologist, Dr. Dunfee, called us into his office and told us that Susan had an incurable kidney disease that neither dialysis nor kidney transplants were feasible to deal with her sickness. He told us that she would have between 1 and 10 years to live. We both were crushed as we now had 2 young sons.

That night, I tried to follow Dad's advice by looking for the answers to life in the Bible. But when I looked, all I saw was a bunch of words that meant nothing to me. A little later that night, the pastor of the church that we occasionally attended called me and asked how we were doing. I told him about the situation and that we were doing terrible. I asked if we could come and see him. When we went to his home in the next day or so, he opened the Bible and shared several verses with us from the book of John and Romans. A couple of verses that I remember that he shared with us were **John 3:16**- *"For God so loved the world that he gave his one and only Son, that whoever believes in him shall not perish but have eternal life."* And **Romans 6:23**- *"For the wages of sin is death, but the gift of God is eternal life in Christ Jesus our Lord."*

What happened next was pretty amazing. In that moment, God opened the hearts of both Susan and me to believe in Him and accept Christ as our Savior. Immediately it was like a huge weight was taken off my shoulders in that while I didn't know what the outcome was going to be or if I was going to be raising our 2 sons on my own, I no longer was doing it alone. It was both very special and timely in that I was able to reconnect with my Mom and Dad to tell them that I loved them and asked their forgiveness for things that they didn't know about my life. I was a new man. Dad died later that year but I was so grateful for the months that we had together.

Over the next several months, Susan went back for continued testing on her kidneys. Little by little it the disease started disappearing and after 6 months it was totally gone from her system. She was healed. We were both very thankful to hear that but still had some trepidation about whether it was totally gone or not. 10 years later, Susan needed emergency surgery. When the ER doctor asked about her medical history, she told him that she had the complex kidney disease. The doctor responded, "That's impossible. If you really had that, you wouldn't be here. Who was your nephrologist?" When we told him that it was Dr. Dunfee, he said, "Dunfee is the best. If he diagnosed you as having it, you had it." Then the ER doctor literally hurried around the emergency room and pointed to Susan, exclaiming, "There's a miracle that happened over there." He then came back to us and said to Susan, "Someone above had their hand on you." We joyfully agreed. One may think that after that, since we had new-found faith and had experienced a miracle, that life would be a bowl of cherries. I would love to tell you that was the case, but that wasn't the case.

When I became a Christian, I thought I knew what that meant based on what I observed growing up. In my mind, I thought there were moral rules that if we obeyed them, we were on track and if we didn't, we weren't. So no more movies and whenever the church doors were open, we were there. It didn't make any difference if one of our boys had a 104 degree temperature, we were there. Since Susan didn't come from the same background that I did, this was all foreign to her and began alienating her. A few years later, we experienced some problems in the church. People were backbiting each other, sharing rumors, and talking behind people's backs, etc. As a result, Susan said to me, "If this is what Christianity is about, why would I want to be a Christian?" She was right in asking that question and it began a new leg of our journey to try to understand it. Unfortunately, we've observed that kind of behavior in churches since then too. I even found myself in the middle of a couple of them trying to 'fix' things. While I felt that I was doing the noble, God-honoring thing, the joy of the Lord began slipping away from me when I would think about church. And it got to the point that Susan didn't even want to go to church.

A few years into my new life of Christianity, I was challenged to think about what I would want to be said about me at the end of my days. I said that I hoped people would say that I tried to live with the 'Attitude of Christ'. So now, this was being put to the test.

In 1999, I was dealing with church issues and also, dealing with some lawsuits that were filed against our company that I felt were totally unfair and unjust. At work in particular, I felt the weight of the world that it was my job to defend us and 'win'. These circumstances just happened prior to my heart attack that I mentioned at the beginning of the book. As a side note, I thankfully have continued to have good heart health since then.

As I said before, it could have been the worst day of my life but turned out to be the best day of it. I was and am grateful that God gave me a tap on the shoulder rather than a life-ending knock on the head. This event began the ending of the first half of my spiritual life.

My life up to this point was about establishing my identity in life. It was based on things that were grounded in pride like my position at work, the home we lived in, the cars we drove . . . things that would prove to others that we were successful. On the outside it all looked pretty good. I was in control and making it happen, so I thought. As you are learning, it wasn't nearly as pretty on the inside. Actually it was somewhat depressing. A wall had been built up between Susan and me. To some degree, I wasn't connecting well with the boys. And our home was only marginally a happy one.

In spite of this, I would like to add that the 1st Half of our Journey is very necessary for each of us. It involves a lot of pride and ego as we "build our box". But as life goes on, we begin to realize that the stuff in our box isn't what brings true meaning to our lives. It's just preparation for the 2nd half of our spiritual journey for people willing to be humbled to learn from their mistakes. Not everyone is willing to open their minds and hearts to the rest of the journey in pursuit of finding Purpose and Joy.

The Steps that follow are the steps that helped me learn to manage stress after my heart attack. They are the Steps that helped me Find Purpose and Joy in Life. Perhaps you may find them to be helpful as well. After the 10 Steps, I'll share the 2nd Half of My Spiritual Journey.

POINTS TO PONDER
- What is your story up until now?
- What have been some of your positive and negative experiences?
- What are you experiencing today... both positive and negative?
- What things would you like to begin changing?

Roger Laidig

Step 1- Destination. Where Do I Want to Go?

"Without vision, the people perish. Begin with the end in mind."

So if you were a pilot in Mishawaka, IN and were preparing to fly to Fort Myers, FL, what is one of the first things that you would do? Wouldn't you prepare a flight plan including charting the course? So after you check the weather, inspect the plane, the fuel, and a lot of other small but important details, up and away you go. All is going well until out of nowhere an unexpected thunderstorm pops up in front of you as you're flying over eastern Kentucky. What would you do? As you evaluate the options, you decide that it would be best if you change course and head southwest for a while to avoid the storm. Now you are heading straight toward New Orleans. While you've always heard that city is a fun place, real life kicks back in.

So what happens next? Since you remember that Fort Myers is where you want to end up, you do the logical thing and re-chart your course. Now you are again heading for your planned destination. After a couple of fuel stops and making a few more course corrections to avert problems, you safely end up in sunny Fort Myers.

You might be wondering, "What does this have to do with finding purpose and joy?" Good question. Let's apply it to our individual journeys in life. As one of many sayings go, "If you don't know where you're going, you'll probably end up somewhere else".

When our oldest son, Ryan, was considering college choices, we visited Taylor University in Upland, IN. During the interview, our Taylor counselor-for-the-day asked Ryan, "What would you like your life to look like in 40 years?" His point was that if you can have a vision for what you want in 40 years, your decision of where and how you get educated can either put you on a course toward achieving your hopes or if you don't consider anything more than the here and now, there is a really good chance that you'll end up somewhere else. I thought that was sage advice.

It was at that point, that the counselor's question probably impacted me more personally than it did Ryan. I began thinking about what things would look like 40 years from then in several aspects of my life. Areas including my marriage, the lives of our children and our future grandchildren, relationships with other people, financial, physical, and emotional well-being, and lots of other things. Most of the things that I thought more deeply about were about people and relationships. The biggest question I had was, "What will my spiritual life be like? Will I feel like I am living with purpose and will my life overflow with joy?"

At that point in time, by most "Christian standards", I would have been thought to be on solid ground as I was an elder and a Sunday School teacher. Outwardly our family looked good. But the truth is that our home was not a happy home. As I mentioned, a wall had been built between Susan and me. Our boys resented me at times. While we would have never split up our home because our commitment when we got married was "for better or worse until death do us part", we were merely living separate lives under the same roof. While I believe I put on a good face, I was dying inside and didn't know what to do about it. I was on my knees begging God to do something, to change Susan and the boys' attitudes toward me . . . 'to change them'.

By the grace of God, I met a counselor that gave me so much insight. After meeting with both Susan and me together and then individually, he helped me understand that Susan didn't feel valued by me. I wasn't giving her the freedom to have "her" feelings and opinions. It's ironic that one of the main reasons that she was attracted to me was that I was somewhat bold, could make decisions fairly quickly, and was confident about life. Well it turns out that it didn't take much time after we got married for her to realize that these "strengths" would become her nightmare.

This awakening helped me understand some teaching that I had heard about earlier in my life . . . ***"Strengths carried to extreme become our weaknesses."*** This might be good for each of us to consider. What are your strengths? Are you quiet? What happens in your relationships if you are 'quiet to extreme'? Are you discerning? What happens if you are 'discerning to extreme'? Are you fun loving? If you are 'fun loving to extreme', how does it affect others? Are you quick and decisive? If you are 'quick and decisive to extreme', how do others respond?

The opening of my mind to this principle began a process that was and still is life changing. I began to realize that the problem wasn't 'them' but rather, it was 'me'. While I could perhaps influence 'them' with my attitude and actions, I could not change them. And I shouldn't have been trying to. Another thing that I started to understand was that I was not a very good listener. Oh I could hear words but the concept of listening with understanding escaped me. Here's how that played out. I would listen for a little while and before too long I would say things like "but", "no", or "you shouldn't feel that way". In other words, I wasn't giving Susan and my boys the freedom to have their own thoughts, feelings, and opinions. And when I used the words listed above, it was like a switch. It just shut them off from me. Our conversations for the most part had been all about me and what I thought, rather than about them and what they thought.

Unfortunately when I started understanding these new concepts, I learned a couple more things. First, I had made so many withdrawals from their emotional bank accounts that walls had been built. And each time I made a withdrawal, it put another block on the wall that became a divide between us. By this time, the wall between Susan and me was so high that we could hardly see or hear each other anymore and all trust had eroded.

Thankfully, the question that the Taylor counselor had asked became a focal point to me. What would I want things to look like in 40 years? Did I hope for a divided and unhappy home like we currently had been experiencing or did I hope for something much better. Wouldn't it be nice if we could have a happy home where we loved and respected each other… one where we would enjoy each other's company? Where fun and joy abounded? Yes, that's exactly what I hoped for!

Now that it was clear in mind as to where I hoped my life and the life of my family should head, it was time to begin developing a flight plan. Father's Day was coming soon so I told my family that I didn't want any gifts. All I wanted was 3 hours of their time so that we could talk about what would make a happy home from their perspectives. This first year we ended up going to downtown Chicago for a few days just to chill out. On Father's Day we ended up at a famous Chicago Pizza Parlor and ordered a deep-dish pizza. Since it took a long time for the pizza to make it to our table, it gave us the perfect opportunity to just talk. I asked them each to share what would make our home a happy one . . . one that they would want to bring friends to. A place that they could trust to come back to no matter what circumstances they may face in life.

After receiving their input that day, I began formulating our family mission statement. Then I encouraged them to make any changes or additions that they would like to see. Throughout that year, we began creating the environment that we all wanted. I could see that much of it had to do with my role as husband, father, and leader of our home. The following two Father's Days we continued to hone in on it. In addition to having a dominant personality, I am also detailed (to extreme at times). So after 3 years our Family Mission Statement seemed to be well established (with far more detail than was necessary). Even so, our journey was off the ground and gaining some speed. Here is the basic mission statement that we agreed on without all the detail as to how we would go about accomplishing it.

OUR FAMILY MISSION STATEMENT
January 10, 2000

"Our family is happy and has fun together. Christ is the center of our home. We all feel secure that we

belong. We support each other in our seen and unseen potential. Our home is a safe haven where there is unconditional love. We show respect, kindness, and consideration for each other. We desire to be a family where we continually grow in mental, physical, social, emotional, and spiritual ways. We discuss and discover all aspects of life including our deepest cares and concerns. We are a family that serves each other and the community. We believe that diversity of race, culture, and temperaments are a gift. We hope to leave a legacy of the strength and importance of families."

By writing this mission statement, it didn't mean that we already were there. But it gave us a much clearer picture as to where we desired to head. Both my family and I have encountered some thunderstorms along the way since then, but knowing where we are heading has and is helping us re-route our course from time-to-time so that we get to where we all really do want to be. My personal hope is that we all can experience a slice of Heaven right here as we are living on Earth. Lives filled with purpose and joy.

How about your life? No doubt that your circumstances and preferences are probably a lot different than mine. Are you happy with where you're at and where you seem to be heading? If so, congratulations! From talking to many people that have experienced some bumps in the road, you may be in the minority. On the other hand, if life just is leaving you with some feelings of void, dryness, and anxiety, perhaps it might be a good time for you to begin thinking about what you hope that your life will look like in 40 or so years.

One of the most important takeaways that I hope you get from this book is this. Today is NOT your destination. It's merely the first day of the rest of your life. Please consider your past but don't mire in it.

15

Roger Laidig

Your history is a great place to think about fond memories. At the same time also review what hasn't turned out well. Then most importantly, begin planning on what you can do differently as you begin anew on the journey ahead of you. ***Remember, Today is the First Day of the Rest of Your Life!***

Where do you want to go and who do you want to be as a person? This is not about what kind of job you will have or how much money you will accumulate. It's about your character and your values. One way of looking at this would be to write your own epitaph. No joking. Down deep inside, how would you really hope that people would remember you? Don't think about the past and the good or bad that you may have done. Just consider what you will have some control over in the days yet to come. Remember, people are forgiving for people that exhibit humility. They love to hear about people that have taken stock of the past and re-ordered their lives. If you are like me, that will include the need to forgive yourself for past mistakes so that you can move forward. At the end of the day, do you realize that forgiveness is available to all of us if we too, are willing to forgive others as well as ourselves?

One real reason it is so important to forgive ourselves as well as others is based on what the Bible spoke to me, that when God said, "Your grace and mercy are real and that Jesus death was fully sufficient to bring forgiveness. And incredibly . . . Even my conscience can be cleansed". 1 John 1:9 says, *"If we confess our sins, he is faithful and just and will forgive us our sins and purify us from all unrighteousness."* And Luke 6:37 says, *"Do not judge, and you will not be judged. Do not condemn, and you will not be condemned. Forgive, and you will be forgiven."*

As a side note, if you get lost on your journey once in a while, don't worry. Many times we uncover and learn about new things for better or worse when we temporarily get off course. The important thing though is to remember where you are heading in the big picture and get 'back on the bike' and start riding again. If your desired destination evolves as you gain more experiences and gain new insights, that too will keep you growing.

Start fresh now. It's a new day!

POINTS TO PONDER
- What would you like to have your life look like in 40 years?
- Have you developed a plan with clear vision as to where you want to be in 40 years?
- Do you see any value you in doing that?
- What's holding you back?

Roger Laidig

Step 2- Is the Choice Really Mine?

"The choice is ours. We all have choices to make. If our choices take us closer to our vision, they are wise choices. If they take us further away from our vision, they are foolish."

As you begin to consider what you would like your life to look like 40 years from now or somewhere down the road, you may be wondering, "Do I really have a choice about this?" You might also be thinking, "Well this is just the way I am and I can't do anything about it."

We all are who we are because of 3 factors:
1. *Our Genetics*- When we were born, we did inherit some traits from our ancestors.
2. *Our Early Environment*- We then gained some of our perspective about life based on the environment that we have been raised in. This can influence how we see conflict, peace, our language, how to deal with adversity, etc.
3. *Our Choices*- *As* we grow older and begin to mature, we have the ability to make choices as to how to approach the circumstances that we find ourselves in. At the end of the day, *Our Choices* are the major contributing factors in determining who we are and who we will become.

When I was born, my **genetics** were flavored with German descent and Germans can be known to be somewhat hardheaded. The **early environment** that I was raised in was an influence of hard work and little play. There was not much joking around. Just get the job done. This worked for me until I went to college. And then for the first time in my life, it was FREEDOM! It was at this point it became **MY choices** about how to do life . . . and I didn't make very good choices through my college years and in my early twenties. It is interesting that as I got older, my genetics and early environment again began influencing my choices, though. Some things I desired to emulate and some, I felt might be better to change.

With certainty, it is known that the most unique characteristic of human beings, is that we are born with the ability to make choices that will affect our lives. Every day we make hundreds if not thousands of little choices. Things like whether to...

- Be nice to somebody (or not)?
- Be helpful to others or selfish?
- Follow-through on commitments you make?
- Speak or be quiet?
- Wear brown or blue socks?
- Borrow money or not?
- Get drunk or not?
- Tell the truth or lie?
- Hang around with a good crowd or bad crowd?
- Follow the crowd?
- Think about what I want my life to look like down the road (or not)?
- And the list goes on and on in literally every waking minute of our life.

GOOD CHOICES AND BAD CHOICES

"Chaotic Life"   **"Purpose and Joy"**

"Chaotic Life"   **"Purpose and Joy"**

Bad choices or good choices?
Confused and trying to go both ways.
A crash down will happen before long.

In these figures, there are 2 walls and a different ladder leaning against each wall. The Left Wall represents steps to a "Chaotic Life", figuratively, or the way you don't want your life to turn out. The Right Wall represents steps to a life filled with "Purpose and Joy", figuratively, or the way you hope your life looks like in 40 years or whatever timeframe you choose.

Good Choices are choices that will take you a step higher on the right ladder toward a life that looks more like 'heaven' as you define it. These are wise choices.

Bad Choices are choices that will take you a step higher on the left ladder toward a life of 'hell'. These are foolish choices.

When your life becomes confusing and you continually mix Good Choices and Bad Choices together, you begin waffling between the two ladders kind of like a lukewarm person and ultimately you crash and hit bottom. This is the kind of life that I was leading in college and the next few years thereafter. While I didn't crash to the very bottom, I became somewhat depressed because I was making choices that were counter to who I thought I wanted to become. I showed "party" on the outside but some "anguish" on the inside. While I wasn't sure where I wanted to go, I was pretty sure I wasn't headed the right direction. As time went on, I began to sense that I wanted to start living on a higher road. This ultimately opened my heart to step through the door, when Christ opened it.

Are you beginning to sense that moving forward toward finding a life filled with purpose and joy starts with your choices?

POINTS TO PONDER
- Do you buy into the statement that your choices will define your future?
- What are 'good choices' that you could be making?
- What are 'bad choices' that you could be making?

- What is holding you back from making all 'good choices'?

Roger Laidig

Step 3- What's the Best Use of My Time?

"The best use of our time is spent in preventing future crises."

Early in my management career at Laidig, Inc., at Christmas one of the employees that was under my supervision gave me a small trophy of a fireman with a plate that said "Fire Chief of the Year". While I believe he meant it to be a compliment based on how busy I was, it made me think. If I was a champion fire fighter, something must be wrong with my leadership abilities. The best leaders prevent crises instead of fighting them.

What is the best use of our time could also be known as good time management. Time management is the act or process of planning and exercising conscious control over the amount of time spent on specific activities, especially to increase effectiveness, efficiency or productivity. There are an abundance of books, classes, workshops, day-planners, and seminars on time management, which teach individuals and corporations how to be more organized and more productive. Time management has become crucial in recent years thanks to the 24/7, busy world in which we live.

PRIORITIES

As you begin thinking about the best use of your time, it's probably a good time to clearly identify your priorities based on where you hope to end up in 40 years or so. Here is one way of doing that.

Remember the wagon wheels from the old 'wild west' movies? Now picture each spoke of the wheel as an aspect of your life. For purpose of this example, each spoke represents a different aspect…

- Spiritual well-being
- Family
- Work and financial well-being
- Physical well-being
- Emotional well-being

These spokes are simply suggestions that seem to be common for a lot of people. If they are not quite on the mark for you, rename them to fit your life.

If you are living a balanced life by paying attention to each facet of your life, the wagon travels smoothly down the road. But if your life gets out-of-whack and you're spending a lot more time in some facets while neglecting others, what happens? The road of life becomes quite bumpy and perhaps rocky at best. So as you consider big picture time management, perhaps it would be a good idea to think about ALL aspects of your life and not just work at whichever you tend to favor.

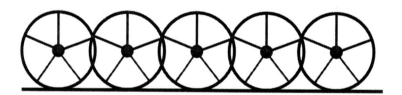

A balanced life runs smoothly down the road.

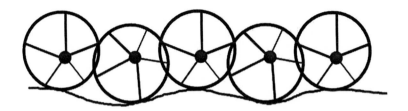

An unbalanced life leads to a chaotic and bumpy road.

FOUR QUADRANTS

Over the years, I've learned about and used various time management systems but as of this time, one has risen above the rest for me. Perhaps you will find it to be of value also. It is the 'Four Quadrants' method that was introduced to me by Stephen Covey in his book, "7 Habits of Highly Effective People."

	Urgent	Non-Urgent
Important	1	2
Non-Important	3	4

In this illustration,

- Q1 (Quadrant 1) represents activities that you spend time on that are both urgent and important
- Q2, activities that are not urgent but important
- Q3, activities that seem urgent but not important
- Q4, activities that are neither urgent or important

This method has been around several years so you may well be familiar with it. If that's the case, this can serve as a way to dust it off and think about how you are using your time . . . a refresher. If this is the first time that you've seen it, hopefully it will give you a new perspective on your use of time.

Here are some questions to ponder...

- What are examples of activities for each quadrant?
- In which quadrant do you think most people spend their time?
- In which quadrant do you spend most of your time?
- Which quadrant would be the best place to use more time?
- How can you find more time to spend in that quadrant?

Quadrant 1 – Activities that are Important and Urgent

Q1 is the quadrant of CRISIS. This quadrant is where most people unwittingly spend a lot of their time. Q1 may be referred to as the quadrant of necessity and contains the tasks that are urgent and important. These are the tasks you have to do or else you will face negative consequences. Usually these are deadline driven and/or time sensitive. On a daily basis, it is inevitable that you will do tasks that fall in Q1. The key is to being able to manage these.

Q1 tasks include:

- Medical emergencies
- Filing your taxes
- Last minute changes
- Tasks that have deadlines

If you feel like you are **firefighting** most of your days, it is a sign that you are spending too much time in this quadrant. You are just doing the things that are crisis oriented. The question is, "How can I get out of this rat race? Hint, you want to shift investing more time in long-term solutions (see Q2).

When I was given the "Fire Chief of the Year" trophy, I was obviously spending far too much time in this quadrant.

Quadrant 2 – Important and Not Urgent

Q2 is the quadrant of PREVENTION. This is THE quadrant where you want to invest most of your time. You may question this because these tasks are not urgent. While that's true, they are all about prevention of future crisis. Q2 tasks should be designed to prevent potential Q1 tasks from ever happening. Tasks in Q2 are in direct alignment with your vision and lead you to where you desire to be 40 years or so from now. They are things you want to achieve in the long-run. Here are a few examples of quadrant two tasks:

- Designing and implementing systems to prevent future crisis at work and home. This is what I needed to do in order to do less firefighting at work.
- Include time for all aspects of your 'wagon wheel' of life
- Scheduling some quiet time to refresh your spiritual and emotional well-being
- Spending time with your family and friends
- Exercising
- Developing and following a budget
- Taking classes outside your job to advance your career

Everyone's goals and dreams are different. What might be a Q2 task for me, might not be for you. Also, do you see that the tasks are non-urgent? This might seem counterintuitive at first. A lot of times we associate things that have a sense of urgency as important, but that is not the case. Your desires and dreams are not running away; they will be right where they are now and there is no urgency to achieving them within a specified timeline. Anything that benefits you in the long run could be considered in Q2.

Quadrant 3 – Not important and Urgent

Q3 is the quadrant of DECEPTION. People often confuse these as being important tasks while in fact they are not. Or people think the task is urgent but it really is not (and thus should belong in Q4).

A common occurrence of mistaking something as important is when someone is asking you to do something that does not directly help you achieve your goals. The key here is being able to say "no" to these people.

An example of this at home came early in our marriage when I played on a softball team with co-workers and friends. That event in and of itself wasn't a problem. The problem was that when the games were over, I allowed my friends to convince me that it was really important to go out for some drinks and fellowship. And because this didn't rate very high on Susan's list, this activity then moved to Q1, a crisis.

Examples of mistaking something as urgent, while they are not, are often sources of distraction. For example,

- Doing things that other people tell you are urgent but they really aren't
- Doing easy things rather than what needs to be done.
- Picking up the phone while you are working
- Constantly checking your email inbox and responding right away.
- Constantly checking Facebook updates
- Continually checking your phone for text messages

Quadrant 4 – Not important and Not Urgent

Q4 is the quadrant of WASTED TIME. It contains the tasks you want to avoid as much as possible. These are time wasters that you want to eliminate. If you could identify all your Q4 tasks and eliminate most of them, you would free up a lot of time you could otherwise invest in quadrant two tasks.

Some examples include doing these things in <u>excess</u>:

- Playing video games
- Watching reruns of your favorite TV shows
- Following the news
- Checking your social media
- Most things that you do in excess

The caveat is that this quadrant can be mistaken as something that shouldn't be part of life, but that is not true. It is really important to have a balanced life between work and your personal life. You need downtime to not get burnt out and that is where Q2 comes into the picture. The challenge is you allocate most of your time to Q2, with just enough of time spent in Q4 to get by.

The real key to effective time management using the Four Quadrants is continually evaluating time that you are spending in Q3 and Q4 and shifting that time to invest it into Q2 activities. This will require discipline and selflessness. It is worth it though because the rewards can be great. Spending more time effectively in Q2 many times will result in…

- Less crises because they have been prevented
- Happier family life because they have become an important part of your time and life.
- More productiveness and job success
- Better health and well-being
- Much less stress in all areas of your life.

So if you want a little short-term joy with little purpose in your life, Q3 and Q4 will help you achieve that.

But if you truly want to discover purpose for your life along with long-term peace and joy, invest time into Q2. Perhaps you will need a true friend or trusted advisor to help you re-arrange your schedule and get on track for much better tomorrows.

Roger Laidig

POINTS TO PONDER

- Do you currently use a time management system and how is it working?
- Which quadrant do you spend most of your time in?
- What kinds of things are you doing that are Quadrant 2 activities?
- What can you change to allow you to spend more time in Quadrant 2?

Step 4- What Should I Spend My Time and Energy On?

"Spend our time and energy on things we can control. In the things we can't control, exercise faith."

In Step 3 we talked about time management and what is the best use of our time. This is a natural transition into Step 4, which is about what we should spend our time and energy on. These two steps could easily be reversed and they do work well together.

Have you spent much time thinking about what are the causes of stress in your life? If you are like most human beings, isn't a lot of our stress self-induced? Why is that? If you step back and examine such situations, doesn't a lot of our worry and anxiety come from things that we have no control over? Here are some examples that you might be able to relate to…

- You tell your friend how to solve a dilemma in their life but they don't listen to a word you say.
- Your favorite sport team blows a game because of what you think is a poor decision by the coach or referee.
- You have diligently prepared and invested in something that has a solid history of good returns, but the economy turns south and you lose big time.
- Your spouse or child doesn't think like you want them to think and it frustrates you to wits end.
- Your boss never seems to appreciate your work.

The list could go on and on. But do you see a common ingredient? Doesn't each one of them involve something that you have no control over?

Do you choose to TAKE RESPONSIBILITY or to BE A VICTIM? I believe that the biggest choice you can make along your journey of life is this one. Take some time to think about this. Do you agree or not? It is your choice. If you don't agree, would you at least consider these thoughts?

VICTIM MENTALITY

While there are exceptions to everything, by and large what does having a 'victim mentality' mean? From BecomeSelfAware.com, "A victim is someone who feels powerless, and is therefore unable to take appropriate action to resolve situations adversely affecting their well-being. Being powerless is learned behavior originating from repeated childhood experiences where core needs were not met adequately. From birth and through early childhood children are unable to provide for themselves basic physiological needs, safety needs, the social needs of belonging, love and affection, and the self-esteem needs of personal worth, social recognition and having a satisfying sense of accomplishment. The victim mentality is characterized by an attitude of blaming and complaining. The secret agenda of blaming and complaining is to manipulate and control others to be responsible for you by rationalizations and excuses."

Does blaming others solve problems? Think for a minute, how do you feel when someone blames you for something? Isn't your immediate and natural reaction to become defensive? And rather than solve the problem, doesn't it actually end up escalating it?

Seeing ourselves as a victim usually ends up in frustration. Frustration happens when we experience blocked goals. And blocked goals are a result of expectations from people or things that we have no control over. Thus, we see ourselves as a victim.

If you recall from a couple of chapters back, when I felt that Susan and the boys were on a different page than I was, my hope was that 'they would change'. That is a shining example of victim mentality. If I had continued to take that approach, how do you think it would have turned out? Our home environment didn't start making a change for the better until I began realizing that I was a big part of the problem. It was time for me to take responsibility rather than blame them.

TAKE RESPONSIBILITY

Taking responsibility is about choosing differently. Learning to take responsibility is a true sign of a person becoming mature, isn't it? If you are interested in growing in this area, here are some action items that will help you.

- Realize that while you can influence others through your actions and attitudes, you cannot change them. The only person that you can change is you. And the change that is most necessary is in your attitude.
- Recognize the victim mentality and victim identity. Stop blaming, complaining and rationalizing why you can't do something.
- Love who you are and do away with the habit of self-judgments and criticism.
- Visualize what you would like your life to look like in 40 or so years driven by honor and integrity.
- Know your values and use them as guidelines for the choices you make and the behavior in which you engage.
- Commit to be loyal to yourself and live by principles that honor, respect and promote well-being for everyone.
- If someone is critical of you, consider it with an open mind. If there is some truth to it, acknowledge it and work on changing. If there is not truth, shake it off and move forward.
- Remember that another person can only make you feel bad if you give them permission to. After all, isn't it simply their opinion? Don't give people the power to dictate how you feel.
- Rather than setting 'goals' on things that you have no control over, just consider them as 'desires' rather than 'goals'. Do your best to positively influence the outcome but have <u>faith</u> that the results will turn out as they are supposed to be.

FORGIVE

- Be forgiving of yourself when you fail to live up to your new standards, particularly at the beginning of this self-transformation.

- Be forgiving of others that have wronged you. Why lose twice? You lost initially when you believed you were wronged. And don't you continue to lose if you hold on to bitterness?
- Don't repay with vengeance. That will just escalate the drama, won't it?

THE POWER OF ONE- Taking responsibility for yourself is just focusing your attention on what is in your control and for the most part, that equates to your attitude. No matter what your circumstances are, even though you can't 'change' others, you can begin to influence them in a positive way through the attitudes you exhibit as you face challenges. This is the POWER OF ONE that we each have if we choose to.

Here are a few quotes from some very bright and recognizable people...

"I am convinced that life is 10% what happens to me and 90% how I react to it. And so it is with you . . . we are in charge of our attitudes."
— Charles R. Swindoll, Pastor and Teacher

"In the long run, we shape our lives, and we shape ourselves. The process never ends until we die. And the choices we make are ultimately our own responsibility." ~Eleanor Roosevelt, Former First Lady

POINTS TO PONDER
- What kinds of things are you spending time worrying about that you have no control over?
- Is 'taking responsibility' more valuable than being a 'victim'? Why?
- Are there any areas in your life that you are feeling like a 'victim?
- How can you begin 'taking responsibility' in those areas?
- What do you think about 'the power of one'?

Finding Purpose and Joy

Step 5- If Someone Loses, Does Anyone Really Win?

"When looking for the best scenario, always strive for a win-win situation."

We have some terrific grandkids and we wouldn't trade them for anything. But when their grandmother, Mimi, plays with them, each of them usually wants to be first . . . the first one to select the game, the one to make the first move, and so on. And then the other ones feel like they lost and express their feelings accordingly. Mimi does a great job of encouraging sharing so they usually get through it fine.

What about any group of people including older kids and even 'adults'? Do even adults want to get their way? Such topics could include things like how to solve a problem, which movie to go to, what color to paint the room, where to go on vacation, or just about anything that involves differences of opinions.

It has been said that comparison and competition when carried to extreme are the two top causes of troubles in relationships. Why do you think that is? Isn't it because of our pride and ego? And when one feels like they have won, how do the others feel? Typically they feel like they lost. Or if one just 'gives in' to appease the other party, sooner or later they are likely to feel like the doormat and develop a loser mentality.

This is a topic that we each may have different perspectives on. Wouldn't it be abnormal if it weren't that way since we all have different genes, backgrounds, and temperaments? One of many blind spots that have been revealed to me over the years is that while outwardly I thought I was pretty neutral, inside, I simply hated to lose.

As I have mentioned before, I thought I was 'right' about a lot of things. Inherently that meant that I thought that others were wrong. My strength of confidence carried to extreme was actually arrogance. And when I had the satisfaction of 'winning' a disagreement, I kind of felt good that the opposing party lost. What do you suppose this did for building trust in my relationships? Well starting at home, if I 'won' something, someone else felt like they lost. And before long, they would retaliate in some way that was consistent with their temperament. It would typically manifest itself by the other party withdrawing or occasionally fighting back verbally. And each time that I did this, it was a withdrawal that I took from their emotional bank account that added a brick or two to the wall that was forming between us.

I write this with regret because during most of the years that I discovered that I was doing this, I professed to be a Christian, was an adult Sunday School teacher, and an elder at our church. I read the Bible regularly, which I continue to believe is our true living water, but somehow missed one of the most important messages that is in it. That is, to love your neighbor as yourself. Although I thought I was doing this, I really wasn't because every time that I won something, someone else lost something. That isn't true love, is it?

Although I was beginning to understand some time ago on my life journey, one of the top lessons that I have been coming to grips with over the past 5 years is that it is not OK to end up with 'win/lose' results . . . as much as it depends on me. It is far better to take the extra time to see if there is a solution that both parties can feel pretty good about and walk away from the table feeling like it ended up being a win-win situation. This approach employs another Covey-ism, 'Fast is slow and slow is fast'. If we try to try to rush through situations, they are very slow to develop. On the other hand, if we take our time to work through situations striving to find win-win solutions, we develop strong bonds of trust that allow us to be able to work through things faster in the future because we trust each other.

When you find yourself involved in a disagreement, have you ever stopped to think that just as you think the other party is wrong, most times, they believe that you are the one that is wrong? And you know what? There is a really good chance that both you and the other party are right about some things and also a really good chance that you are both wrong about some things.

How many logs are there?

I see three!   I see four!

So how many logs are there? It depends which side you're standing on, doesn't it? Interestingly, this is exactly how a lot of debates and misunderstandings begin. The next thing you know, the left guy says to the right guy, "You're crazy!" and the right guy responds, "Well, you're dimwitted and can't count." And with that, they hit each other's 'fear buttons' and the fight is on.

If they would have just slowed down a little so that they could listen to each other and put their feet in the other person's shoes, they would realize that there is truth from both perspectives. But if they don't, they would probably walk away both feeling disrespected by the other person with a little more distance put between them.

Occasionally though you may encounter situations that even after taking much time to find a win-win solution or come to an agreement, it just doesn't happen. In such cases, please consider that simply agreeing to disagree with an agreeable spirit is the best way to handle the situation. ***Wouldn't the world be a much better place that if we find ourselves in circumstances that we can't find an agreeable solution, we simply agree to disagree and still be respectful to one another.***

What this signifies is that we recognize that the other party sees the situation differently through their glasses and that is OK. It doesn't necessarily mean that we need to be best friends. As far as it is up to us, we will treat them with dignity regardless of how they respond. Our attitude and actions are the only things that we can control. Won't this also give the highest probability of something good coming out of the situation? And what will this say about our character?

What I am finding is that when this approach is taken, over the course of time, we will end up seeing that there is a lot that we do agree on. Then we can make the highest and best decisions by looking at problems from all angles and bringing the best big picture solutions to the top, which is the ultimate Win-Win.

POINTS TO PONDER
- In relationships, why do we naturally want to 'win'?
- When we want to 'win', how is that likely to affect trust building in a relationship?
- Is it worthwhile to take the extra time to try to end up with a 'win-win' solution?
- When win-win just isn't happening, how do you feel about agreeing to disagree but doing it with dignity?

Step 6- Why Do We Have 2 Ears and 1 Mouth?

"Always try to understand another person's perspective before sharing our perspective. See both sides."

Reckless words, spoken hastily and without thinking, inflame many conflicts. "Reckless words pierce like a sword, but the tongue of the wise brings healing" (Proverbs). Although we may seldom set out deliberately to hurt others with our words, sometimes we do not make much of an effort not to hurt others. We simply say what comes to mind without thinking about the consequences. In the process, we may hurt and offend others, which only aggravates conflict.

It's been said that since we all have 2 ears and one mouth, if we use them in that proportion, we'll have much richer relationships. There is another saying that goes like this, "A person doesn't care how much you know until they know how much you care". Think about it for a moment. Do you think that these statements are true? Is there a connection between these two thoughts? It seems to me that the connection is that when we truly listen to others with understanding, they begin to believe that we really do care about them. And then they become interested in what we think as well. The result is trust being built and the relationship being enhanced.

Many times when we have an issue with another person, if we decide to approach them, isn't it natural to want to just let them know how we feel? Because there is a conflict, what we say probably will come across as a criticism or attack on the other person since it's obvious that they see things differently, right? Then if you do that, what typically happens next? Don't most humans get a bit defensive when they feel like they are being criticized or attacked? Your action likely prompts them to react back as a defense mechanism. The next thing you know, you're volleying barbs back and forth in a fashion that escalates because of emotion. You end up blaming each other because 'they just won't listen' and the original issue blows up, gets personal, and you may even forget what the original issue was. In his book, "The DNA of Relationships", Gary Smalley refers to this as 'the fear dance'.

So how do you get out of this 'dance'? Well someone needs to step up, take responsibility, and become 'the adult' in this situation. While that's a topic that could be expanded on greatly, in simple terms it means that one party realizes that blaming each other is going nowhere fast. So at some point, one needs to step back and take responsibility for becoming the initiator of moving toward a solution. It means putting one's pride and ego aside and stepping forward with humility to really take the time to understand fully where the other person is coming from.

But wouldn't it be much better to prevent such problems? But how? Now is probably a good time to introduce the "PAUSE BUTTON". With my temperament, I rarely, if ever, hold grudges. My challenge early on was that if I thought my fear button was being pushed, I would (over) react immediately. Shortly thereafter I would be very remorseful because I knew better but by that time, the damage was done. After wrestling with this probably for years, one of the authors that I have mentioned earlier probably was responsible for me realizing that I had a PAUSE BUTTON.

My PAUSE BUTTON is on the side of my knuckle of my left index finger. So for me to activate my PAUSE BUTTON to put my mind and emotions in neutral, all I would have to do is use my left thumb and press my PAUSE BUTTON. In fact, when I knew I was heading into a conversation that had a chance to be contentious, I would physically use my ink pen and draw a pause button on that knuckle ahead of time. It has helped me a lot since I learned about doing that but unfortunately there are still occasions that I forget about the pause button or completely miss it with my thumb when I'm trying to hit it.

When done effectively, the idea is to simply stop and think before acting or reacting.

So if you occasionally find yourself reacting inappropriately, you too may want to establish or re-establish your pause button. It could be on your index knuckle like mine. It could be on your chin, your ear, or the end of your nose. It's your button so it's your choice. Before long you might even start having fun with it. Sometimes if I knew I was heading into a potentially highly charged meeting, I put a button on both of my index fingers to double my chances of hitting one or the other.

Another way to prevent fear dances or conflicts I learned from Stephen Covey in his "7 Habits" book. He calls it 'Seek First to Understand, Then to Be Understood'. Elvis Presley even must have got this. When I visited Graceland one time, I noticed an Elvis quote on a stone that read "Don't judge another person until you have walked a mile in their moccasins." Maybe he even sang about it. I never much listened to the words of his songs so I really don't know.

My cousin, Jack Laidig, who has been a customer service representative and co-worker of mine for years at Laidig, Inc. provided the best real life example of this approach time after time. When a customer contacts any customer service department, it's rarely because they want to tell them how great their company and products are. Don't they usually make contact because they are upset and many times irritable because they are having problems? So here is how Jack always handled the situation. He first would sincerely say to the customer something like this...

"It sounds like you have a serious problem that you're facing. I want to know everything about it. I also want you to know that my job isn't done until you are completely satisfied. Please tell me everything about your situation with full detail so that I can make sure that I understand what you are experiencing. Is this approach OK with you?"

How do you think the angry customer typically responds? With very rare exception, they immediately become very cooperative. Why is that? It's because they immediately begin believing that Jack cares about them and it starts building a strong bond of trust. Then together they become a 'team' to resolve the problems together with full openness and honesty on both sides and they come up with the highest and best solution. It's like magic. It's a true win-win situation. And Laidig's best repeat customers are ones that actually have had problems and have been handled this way. It's 'Seeking First to Understand, and Then to be Understood' in action.

Can this magic also happen in our everyday relationships? Sure, if at least one party chooses to be the mature one, the adult. Here's how humans usually work. When we are bothered by something, it begins building up inside of us. As time goes on, we begin feeling pressure like a teapot ready to blow off steam.

So when one of the parties decides to take responsibility and listen with empathy, which means with full understanding, it's like slowly lifting the lid off the teapot so that the steam can gradually release. And then when the pressure is all gone, the probabilities are much greater that the other party will then ask you what your perspective is. Trust starts building and the chances of resolving your initial conflict are also increased significantly because you both feel like you have been valued and understood.

Dialog rather than discussion. Whether in an individual or group setting, a great way to create an environment for understanding is to intentionally 'dialog' rather than 'discuss' things. While it may be semantics, in the context that I am about to describe, I have found it to be a game changer.

For the purpose of this concept, to 'discuss' things means that we each bring our own agendas and our goal is to prove to the other person that we are right and they are wrong. The problem is that when we approach conversations this way, we have no desire to listen and understand the other perspectives. We are continually thinking how we can get our points to stick. The result is defensiveness and people walk away only further entrenched and solidified in their own thinking. Rarely does anything good come out of it.

Dialog, on the other hand, is a whole different approach. The adult encourages others to freely share their thoughts. Everyone is considered an equal so there is much respect for one another. The tone is one of listening fully to each other to understand each person's perspective. There is to be no judging or criticizing . . . just listening to understand. And over time, the highest and best ideas begin to float to the top. The probability of all parties embracing the outcome becomes much greater because each person at least feels that they have been heard and included fully in the conversation. The chance of win-win is much more likely to occur and brilliant decisions are made.

Again, to build truly strong and enduring relationships, 'Fast is slow, and slow is fast'. And it reduces stress and anxiety to an astonishing degree.

So the bottom line is we all have 2 ears and 1 mouth. We need to use them in that order and that proportion. Then purpose and joy will prosper in our lives. True friendships grow much deeper as well. I must tell you that while I fully understand the value of this, I continue to need to be reminded of it. It's part of the journey. Maybe it's part of yours as well.

"Even a fool is thought wise . . . and discerning if he holds his tongue." Proverbs 17:28

"Everyone should be quick to listen, slow to speak, and slow to become angry…" James 1:19

POINTS TO PONDER
- Why do we want to just tell another how we feel or how we have been wronged before listening?
- What prevents you from truly listening with understanding?
- Is it worth the time to slow down to truly listen to one another rather than just trying to fast forward through it?
- Would it be of value to you to have a 'pause button'? What would your pause button look like?

Step 7- Look for the good in others

"Look for the good in others. Their strengths help fill in the gaps of our own shortcomings."

Why is it that most people find it much easier to see what is wrong with another person that what is right with them? Is it a result of our pride and ego? Does it indicate that we are so insecure that in order to feel OK about ourselves, we feel the need to put another down? Really think about it. What causes us to approach life in this way?

As you look at this picture above inside of the black frame, what do you see? Most people will see and point out the dark spot.

So the question is, "Can you see that it's really a nice white picture but just happens to have a little dark spot in it?" Isn't that pretty much how we view other people . . . our spouse, our kids, our co-workers, our friends, and definitely our enemies? We tend to only see their 'black spots', rather than all of the white (good) in them.

I mentioned earlier in this book that when I was in my 20's, for some reason I thought that if you saw things differently than me, obviously you were wrong. Unbelievable, right? But have you ever felt that way? If another person doesn't agree with you there must be something wrong with them. In fact, it's a little bit hard to see what value they might have if they don't agree with you. And it may even be difficult to be friends with them. Meanwhile, guess what, they probably are thinking the very same thing about you. Isn't this part of what causes the 'fear dance' in our relationships?

Life is teaching me that there are so many tragedies that happen when we hold so tightly to our own views.

1. If everyone thought like you, what wouldn't get done? When I started just looking around and began to see things like amazing bridges and skyscrapers being built, I started to see that if everyone thought like I did, those kinds of things never would have happened. The same is true when I think about a surgeon performing a procedure. What about people that have the ability to stand at a machine all day to do a particular manufacturing process? I couldn't do any of those things. These are just a few of a multitude of examples that could be listed.

2. Since we all have different temperaments and skill sets, what is someone else able to do that perhaps you wouldn't or couldn't do? Perhaps it's manual labor, mental labor, working behind the scenes, being at the podium, doing repetitive jobs, being flexible to do several different things, and so on.

3. When we just focus on what's wrong with other people, do you believe that they think we value them? And if that happens, is it likely that they will see your value? The biggest reveal that I finally came to realize is that my wife, Susan, didn't feel like I valued her. And though I was blinded and didn't feel that, she was absolutely right.

4. When we don't value other people's opinions or skills whether we think they are absurd or not, we lock ourselves out of so much learning. When I finally started truly valuing Susan's thinking, particularly when it was different than mine, I began seeing how brilliant she is. She was right about so many things. Husbands typically see their wives as nagging at times. Perhaps wives feel the same thing in reverse. What I am learning is that Susan is a special gift that I have been blessed with because she is the one person that knows me best. And she was able to point out blind spots that I had/have that others wouldn't see or didn't have the courage to help me understand. As I learn more and more to check my pride at the door, I now see what a beautiful 'white page' that Susan is in my life.

5. I'm sure that you can come up with many more tragedies that happen when you take time to think about not valuing other people. Are there any people in your life that may not feel valued by you?

I believe that all of us were created for a reason and purpose. None of us are an accident. Even when a person is created with limitations, is it possible that their big picture purpose is to help others learn to express their gifts of caring as well as the development of other attributes? When we look for the good in others, doesn't everyone have the best chance of winning? And by winning, I mean finding their true purpose in life.

Now if the foot should say, "Because I am not a hand, I do not belong to the body," it would not for that reason stop being part of the body. And if the ear should say, "Because I am not an eye, I do not belong to the body," it would not for that reason stop being part of the body. If the whole body were an eye, where would the sense of hearing be?

If the whole body were an ear, where would the sense of smell be? But in fact God has placed the parts in the body, every one of them, just as he wanted them to be. If they were all one part, where would the body be? As it is, there are many parts, but one body.

The eye cannot say to the hand, "I don't need you!" And the head cannot say to the feet, "I don't need you!" On the contrary, those parts of the body that seem to be weaker are indispensable, and the parts that we think are less honorable we treat with special honor. And the parts that are un-presentable are treated with special modesty, while our presentable parts need no special treatment. But God has put the body together, giving greater honor to the parts that lacked it, so that there should be no division in the body, but that its parts should have equal concern for each other. If one part suffers, every part suffers with it; if one part is honored, every part rejoices with it. 1 Corinthians 12

POINTS TO PONDER
- Why do we typically see what's wrong with other people instead of what's right with them?
- Why does this approach usually end up in a 'fear dance?'
- What can you change to begin looking for the good in others?
- What big picture effect will that have on how you see yourself?

Step 8- Try the Platinum Rule

"Treat others as they want to be treated."

You probably have heard of the 'Golden Rule". You know, the one that says, "Do unto others as you would have them do unto you". At first glance, most of us would say, "Sure, I know that and it's probably a really good way to live." That's certainly what I thought. So you might be surprised to learn that this may be the **worst advice** I ever tried to follow when I took it at face value. You see, here's the way I interpreted the Golden Rule when we first got married. Since I like to go to sporting events and since I was to do to Susan as I would want done to me, then naturally I should take her to sporting events. If I like it when the toilet is up, I'll just leave it up each time because that is how I would want it done . . . and on and on. Are you surprised that each time I used this approach, it caused Susan and me to grow just a little bit further apart? Have you ever treated other people the way that you would want to be treated only to find that it caused them to resent you a bit? Or do you suppose it ever has happened and you just didn't realize it?

The big problem with living out the Golden Rule as I did is that it's all about me. And it doesn't really take into consideration what the other person truly wants. When one does it this way to a large extent, they soon are viewed as being selfish or uncaring. The amazing thing is that when I treated others as I wanted to be treated, I was happy since I was so blind to what it was doing to others, particularly my wife. Another example was with our boys. I liked to run 10K's and other types of running races. So when we went on vacation, in the true spirit of treating them the way I would want to be treated, I encouraged them to run. In fact, on one vacation, we had gone the whole vacation without them running one time. So before we ended up back at home,

I stopped at the local middle school and 'encouraged' them each to run around the track at least once. Even though this happened over 25 years ago, I still hear about it. Now they just laugh (at me) when we talk about it.

So does this mean that we should throw the Golden Rule out the window? No, not at all. Here's what I believe it really means. What I am learning about humanity is that we all want to be valued and understood. I want to be valued and understood. So if I truly want to do unto others as I would have them do unto me, I should take the time to value them. This means to listen to them with empathy, to try to walk a mile in their moccasins, and to understand their perspective. That is how I like to be treated and I'm pretty sure that is how we all want to be treated. At the same time, we need to see value in ourselves too. This is the only way we can truly value others too.

So what is The Platinum Rule? While I am not sure who coined the phrase, 'The Platinum Rule', it is actually The Golden Rule better defined. Or as I have heard it said, it's the Golden Rule on steroids. It implies, "Do unto others as they would want done unto them" or shortened, "Treat others as **they** want to be treated". Many times our biggest problem is that we really don't know how others want to be treated because we're all made up differently and come from different backgrounds. We've made different choices to lead us to who we are today.

This would be a good time to reflect back on the steps to finding purpose and joy that we have already covered. If we think about where we desire to head in life and how we would like to be remembered, perhaps we . . .
- Should think about the choices we make and their potential consequences.
- Spend more of our time desiring to truly understand other people, particularly those that are closest to us.
- Tend to create win-win situations rather than just win my way.

- Listen to others to truly understand their perspectives without judgment. Just listen. Our turn to talk will come later and be received much better.
- Look for the good in others rather than the bad. Doing so causes them to believe that we really do care about them. It also increases trust. And trust in the very foundation of true love.
- Remember that in relationships, "Fast is Slow and Slow is Fast".

If we truly want to live out the Platinum Rule and develop great relationships, it is not only good for others but good for your spirit as well. And it will cause you to draw closer to your purpose and bring joy into your life. Anxiety begins to disappear.

POINTS TO PONDER
- Has the traditional Golden Rule ever gotten you into trouble?
- What keeps you from treating others the way they want to be treated?
- Why is learning to listen with empathy a key part of being able to employ the Platinum Rule?
- What do the Platinum Rule and building trust have in common?

Finding Purpose and Joy

Step 9- Is the Sky Really Falling?

"Things are seldom as good as they seem or as bad as they seem. Keep moving forward."

I believe that I first started thinking about this question after reading Richard Carlson's "Don't Sweat the Small Stuff and It's All Small Stuff". Got a stress case in your life? Of course most do. Without question, many of us have mastered the neurotic art of spending much of our lives worrying about a variety of things all at once. His point is that we will live much more stress free lives if we will step back and realize that things are rarely as good as they seem or as bad as they seem. In making this statement, I want to acknowledge that occasionally some things that happen can be life changing and some tragic. Those situations are not what this statement is referring to.

The statement, ***"Things are rarely as good as they seem or as bad as they seem"*** is in reference to most things that happen in our lives that we may tend to over-react to. This is about worry, stress, and anxiety that we self-inflict into our lives that cause us to feel like we're living in chaos.

In addition to Susan's kidney disease and my heart attack, there is one other time that stands out as seeming really bad but turned out to be really good for me in my journey. After graduating from college and grad school, I worked for a large corporation in various aspects of engineering and manufacturing. Since I was sensing that this was not where I wanted to spend my career, I pursued what I thought was a dream. That dream was to build houses. People warned me that there were down sides to becoming a home builder but I chose to ignore them. But man were they right. After a few years of building approximately 30 homes and co-managing a real estate company, I realized that God apparently didn't design me to be a homebuilder. It was very taxing getting up early each morning to make sure that my subcontractors were where they were supposed to be when they were supposed to be there, then dealing with mind changing of customers, finding out that the plumber put the wrong color stool in the bathroom, and so on. Then at night, I had to turn my cap and work with potential customers assuring them what a great experience building their dream home would be.

It turned out to be very exhausting. I began strongly disliking this career. Ironically it was fortunate for me that the interest rates escalated to approximately 18% at that time and home building came to a virtual standstill. It was then that I interviewed for a position at Laidig, Inc. to become the manager and developer of a newly forming industrial division. To do that job effectively would benefit from experiences in engineering, manufacturing, construction, and sales. And what do you know. That was exactly my background. The result was a 30-year career at Laidig, Inc. that I was and am very grateful for.

When I thought the sky was falling when I was building homes, it wasn't at all. It was just great preparation for a career that fit me extremely well. I learned more about what I was good at and enjoyed and also more about what didn't fit me so well.

Stop for a minute. Are you worrying about anything right now? Depending on who you talk to, you'll hear that approximately 90% of the things that we worry about never happen. Of course when I told my wife, Susan, that, she responded, "Well there you have it, now you know why I worry."

One way of evaluating things that we may worry or be anxious about is to ask these questions...
- Really, will it have impact or consequences 1 hour, 1 day, 1 month, or 1 year from now? The shorter the time, shouldn't there be less concern?
- What are you worrying about? A ball game? The clothes you wear? The things you eat? Am I good enough? So and so has wronged me. Should I forgive them?

- But most importantly, ask yourself this question, "Do I have any control over the outcome?" That's a big one. If you do have some control or influence, do what you can and should do . . . and not more and not less. Then think about it, if you don't have any control or ability to influence the situation, what good is 'worry' doing? Aren't those areas where it's time to have faith?

If you are a person of Biblical faith, what does the Bible mean when it says things like "Don't worry about tomorrow, don't worry about the clothes you wear or the food you eat, cast your cares on me, be anxious for nothing."? There is much instruction for us as to how to deal with such circumstances. Doesn't it really boil down to faith? This is not intended to put you on a guilt trip, but it is something to give very serious consideration to, isn't it? Peace is available to each of us.

Phil. 4:6-7 "Do not be anxious about anything, but in everything, by prayer and petition, with thanksgiving, present your requests to God. And the peace of God, which transcends all understanding, will guard your hearts and your minds in Christ Jesus."

How much more peace and joy would you experience if you were able to simply appreciate being alive, keep your emotions (especially anger and dissatisfaction) in proper perspective, and cherish other people as the unique miracles they are? An owner's manual of the heart is free and available to you, and if you follow the directions, you will be a happier, more harmonious person. Remember Step 2, it's your choice.

POINTS TO PONDER
- What kinds of things might you over-react to?
- How does this over-reaction affect you . . . and others?
- We are instructed to 'Be anxious for nothing' and to be 'thankful in everything'. Why do we get this exactly backward a lot of times?
- What can you change that will help you to 'Be anxious for nothing' and to be 'thankful in everything'?

Step 10- Don't ever stop learning

"Always continue to develop your mind through continued learning."

Earlier in this book, I made the statement that the older I get and the more I learn, the more I realize that there is so much that I have yet to learn. And to me, that's what makes getting up each day exciting. To stimulate your mind a bit, think about these things:

- How and when did the native Indians make their way to the Americas?
- When 1 sperm cell and 1 egg unite they multiply into approximately 15 trillion unique and purposeful cells every time a baby is conceived.
- The biggest star discovered by science as of now is Canus Majoris. So to put it in perspective – if the Earth was a golf ball, Canus Majoris would be the height of Mt. Everest. Mt. Everest is almost 6 miles above sea level, the highest point on the planet. 7 quadrillion Earths would fit inside Canus Majoris. That's enough Earths to cover the entire state of Texas in golf balls 22 inches deep.

This list of things could go on and on. The point isn't that we need to learn everything there is to know. Rather, perhaps we should ask ourselves, "Are the things that we have learned and accepted as reality up to this point in our lives the way it really is . . . or is there a chance that there may be other ways of looking at things that may reveal truths that we have never seen or considered before?" When we have a disagreement with others or hold on tight to what we have learned in the past as being the right way or the only way, when we consider the grand scope of the universe, aren't we pretty arrogant if we think we have all the answers? Would it be worthwhile to put our pride to the side and instead, humble ourselves by being open to new learning, to listen to other view points, and to value every human recognizing they each person is a miracle born from our creator whether they are like us or not. Or whether they agree with us or not?

No matter where any of us are at, we need to remember that our journey is not over. Why not open our minds to reading and listening to keep our minds sharp for continued learning? And when we look around at other people, we may tend to judge them as if this is their destination. It is not. And today is not your or my final destination. Finding purpose and joy can be in your future. It's your choice . . . with help from above. We're on this journey together.

POINTS TO PONDER
- Why is important to continually remind yourself that you are not at your final destination?
- Is it important to keep learning and growing? Why?
- Specifically, what are some things that you are sure that you don't know all about, that if you learned more, it could be life changing?
- What steps will you take right now that will put you on the path of growing in that area?

The Second Half of My Spiritual Journey

The 2nd half of our spiritual journey has nothing to do with our age. Unfortunately it usually takes a tragedy or near tragedy to get our attention. Or perhaps we just hit a wall in life when we begin asking, is this all there is? Is this really what life is about? When we truly arrive at this point, then we begin to realize that we are not in control nor do we need to be. It begins at the point that we re-evaluate what is really important to us. We no longer have to 'win' or 'defend' ourselves. We become comfortable in our own skin and no longer feel that we need to prove our worth to others. Most people are typically not capable of giving up the reigns or the need to feel like they are in control of things on their own. That is why it seems to take a really hard event in our lives to begin this process. It is the time that we begin trusting the sovereignty of God and having faith that His plan is far better than our plan particularly when it doesn't coincide with our plan. It's a hard transition. Some people never reach this point. For those that do, it takes a whole lot of stress out of daily life and life actually becomes more enjoyable.

The 2nd half of my journey probably started after my heart attack. For years, while it may not have looked like it on the surface, I felt that I needed to be in control in order to achieve the outcomes that I desired. When things weren't turning out how I thought they should I would feel a lot of tension in my body, particularly my neck and shoulders. I sometimes would become irritable and not easy to be around. For years before and then even after my heart attack, Susan would encourage me to loosen my grip and allow the process of life to solve some of the problems that I thought that I had to solve. I knew she was right but still had a hard time letting go for fear that things wouldn't turn out right if I did.

It was during this time that I began re-evaluating my past experiences and then opening my mind to new ways of looking at things. I began trying to more proactively understand other people's points of view. Was there a chance that maybe things weren't really the way that I thought that they were?

It has taken years since 1999 and more difficult circumstances to begin to die to myself and begin to question the 'truths' that I learned or assumed based on past environments or cultures that I had been in. One of those areas was the church and my spiritual well-being. I mentioned earlier that when Susan saw backbiting and so on going on in the church, she said, if this is what Christianity is all about, why would I want to be a Christian? That question haunted me so I decided to put the church cultures that we had experienced on the shelf temporarily and re-examine this whole Christianity thing.

Earlier in the book, I mentioned that I wanted to be remembered by others as a guy that tried to live with the 'Attitude of Christ'. So now, if I was really serious about this, what is the 'Attitude of Christ'? I believe that His attitude is best defined in these references:

- **Matt 22: 37-40** Jesus replied: "'Love the Lord your God with all your heart and with all your soul and with all your mind.' This is the first and greatest commandment. And the second is like it: 'Love your neighbor as yourself.' All the Law and the Prophets hang on these two commandments."

- **Gal 5:22-23** But the fruit of the Spirit is love, joy, peace, patience, kindness, goodness, faithfulness, gentleness and self-control. Against such things there is no law.

What I had been observing in some church cultures were things including:
- People disrespecting the pastor that was called to their church not because he was in sin but rather because he wasn't performing according to their preferences

- Christians judging, backbiting, gossiping, and talking behind fellow Christian's backs
- Jealousy between churches
- Christian theologians publicly criticizing other Christian theologians when they didn't agree with one another
- People in the pews out of joint when their preferences weren't met
- Churches that are inward focused and their only friends are other Christians. How does that enhance the great commission?
- Shying away from the people of lesser means
- The divorce rate among Christians is no different than it is among those that don't profess to be Christians

In *Pastors at Greater Risk*, H. B. London, Jr. writes about some truly surprising trends about pastors:

- 80% believe the pastoral ministry affects their families negatively.
- 90% feel they're inadequately trained to cope with ministry demands.
- Ministry leaders are equally likely to have their marriage end in divorce as general church members.
- The clergy has the second highest divorce rate among all professions.
- 56% of pastors' wives say they have no close friends.
- 52% of pastors say they and their spouses believe that being in pastoral ministry is hazardous to their family's wellbeing and health.
- 45.5% of pastors say they've experienced depression or burnout to the extent that they needed to take a leave of absence from ministry.
- 70% do not have someone they consider a close friend.

What is wrong with this picture? Isn't the first foundation of the Bible to 'Love the Lord your God with all your heart and with all your soul and with all your mind'? And isn't the second one to 'Love your neighbor as yourself.'? And to do the first one is manifested in part by doing the second one.

Isn't this heartbreaking? It's no wonder that people on the outside believe that Christians are hypocrites. And is it any wonder that many 'Christians' are devoid of purpose and joy?

So does this mean that I am against Christianity? **By no means**. But it seems obvious that much of the time Christianity as a 'religion' seems to be missing the mark by a mile, doesn't it?

Wouldn't it be far more effective if we Christians, did Christianity as a 'lifestyle' instead?

To be clear, I am not against the church. I still believe church can be the hope of the world if we congregants live as Christ commands us to. It takes personal responsibility from each one to look at the logs in our own eyes rather than blame others.

For the last few years, I've stepped away from church ministry to evaluate what I believe has been transpiring. It is my desire to do this with humility in my heart because I, too, have been part of the problem. I felt both Susan and God encouraging me to let go of the tight reins that I was holding as I was trying to help solve the problems in my own strength. I was in great need of getting over myself. So in this part of my journey, for the first time in a long time, I am feeling free to rejoice in God's goodness by trusting in His sovereignty that even though some things didn't go the way "I" thought they should, God was in control and has a master plan that I wasn't able to see. But now, by faith, I have no need to be anxious about those things anymore. This has been a huge factor in feeling the nudging of Susan and the Holy Spirit to write this book. I now have the time and am doing it with joy in my heart. And I believe that our marriage relationship is the best that it ever has been.

Another thing that this process is helping me to realize is that the other people that I may have disagreed with are also going through their journey in life. They are not at their destination either and these circumstances are a necessary part of their journey.

James 1:2-4 says, "Consider it pure joy, my brothers and sisters, whenever you face trials of many kinds, because you know that the testing of your faith produces perseverance. Let perseverance finish its work so that you may be mature and complete, not lacking anything."

This should give us great comfort in knowing that the trials that we face are really opportunities that God is allowing us to learn and grow through to become more mature. And this is a great big step toward finding Purpose and Joy.

POINTS TO PONDER

- Do you think that you are still in the first half of your spiritual journey?
- Are you willing to re-examine things from the past that you have simply accepted because you were told "this is the way it is"?
- Are you fearful of doing this?
- The second half requires total honesty and humility. Are you ready to begin opening yourself to that process? Why or why not?

What about Your Journey?

If you read this book to this point, thank you for your diligence! You're almost done.

I believe that The Steps that are laid out in this book are 'lifestyle' action steps that reflect the Attitude of Christ. Think back over the Steps. It's not for me to be your conscience. Rather, my hope is that you will at least consider them. If you don't agree with what is written, it's no problem from my point of view. We can still hang out and be friends as far as I'm concerned. The bottom line is that your journey is for you and God to work out.

As I said when I told you about my journey, I tried to become a Christian in my own strength and couldn't make it happen. And because of that, no matter where you are on your spiritual walk, I'm not trying to pressure you to become a Christian or trying to say that you're not where you need to be as a Christian. I don't know the motives of your heart. That is between you and God. When God opens the door to your heart, it's **your choice** if you want to walk in. No man can do that for you or convince you that you should. It's your responsibility and no one else's. If you are interested in developing a relationship with God and if you will open yourself to studying the Bible, it promises to speak to you as no man can. If you already acknowledge that you have accepted Jesus into your heart, the Bible is there for your continued growth as well.

"For the word of God is quick, and powerful, and sharper than any two edged sword, piercing even to the dividing asunder of soul and spirit, and of the joints and marrow, and is a discerner of the thoughts and intents of the heart." Hebrews 4:12

"Therefore, I urge you, brothers and sisters, in view of God's mercy, to offer your bodies as a living sacrifice, holy and pleasing to God—this is your true and proper worship. Do not conform to the pattern of this world, but be transformed by the renewing of your mind. Then you will be able to test and approve what God's will is—his good, pleasing and perfect will." Romans 12:1-3

Have you ever wondered if the verse in Matthew 10:30 is actually true? *"And even the very hairs of your head are all numbered."*
Just think about our DNA. We can be identified uniquely and individually by just one strand of our hair. God knows us individually and He gives great promises to each one of us.
Jeremiah 29:11-13- "For I know the plans I have for you," declares the Lord, "plans to prosper you and not to harm you, plans to give you hope and a future. Then you will call on me and come and pray to me, and I will listen to you. You will seek me and find me when you seek me with all your heart."

You have already lived a number of years. Remember that today is not your destination. It's time to start fresh. It's the first day of the rest of your life. Are you willing to use your past experiences along with acting on new lessons that you learn, to help you develop a new way of thinking? If you are, I hope that you will consider where you are at spiritually. And then with God's help, invest yourself by learning new habits and choices that will help you in your journey toward "Finding Purpose and Joy in Your Life".

It would be a good idea to ask a friend that you trust and have observed to be walking in the light, to join with you in helping you on your journey.

If you are interested in:
- The 10 Steps to Finding Purpose and Joy, see exhibit A
- Practical Christianity Bible verses that support the Steps that I have suggested in this book, see Exhibit B
- Suggested books and videos, see Exhibit C

Roger Laidig

Blessings to you! May your journey ahead help you find Purpose and Joy! There is reason for lots of hope in your relationships and life in general.

POINTS TO PONDER
- Have you experienced or are you experiencing any traumatic circumstances in your life?
- Have you kind of 'hit a wall' where you are wondering is this really it? Is this really what life is about?
- Can you see that today is not your destination and your future can start fresh and anew?
- Who do you trust that you could ask to join with you to step positively into the future?
- If you desire to find Purpose and Joy, what will be the next steps that you will take starting now?

Finding Purpose and Joy

Exhibit A

10 STEPS TO FINDING PURPOSE AND JOY

Step 1- Destination. Where Do I Want to Go? "Without vision, the people perish. Begin with the end in mind."

Step 2- Is the Choice Really Mine? "The choice is ours. We all have choices to make. If our choices take us closer to our vision, they are wise choices. If they take us further away from our vision, they are foolish."

Step 3- What's the Best Use of My Time? "The best use of our time is spent in preventing future crises."

Step 4- What Should I Spend My Time and Energy On? "Spend our time and energy on things we can control. In the things we can't control, exercise faith."

Step 5- If Someone Loses, Does Anyone Really Win? "When looking for the best scenario, always strive for a win-win situation."

Step 6- Why Do We Have 2 Ears and 1 Mouth? "Always try to understand another person's perspective before sharing our perspective. See both sides."

Step 7- Look for the good in others. "Look for the good in others. Their strengths help fill in the gaps of our own shortcomings."

Step 8- Try the Platinum Rule: "Treat others as they want to be treated."

Step 9- Is the Sky Really Falling? "Things are seldom as good as they seem or as bad as they seem. Keep moving forward."

Step 10- Don't ever stop learning "Always continue to develop your mind through continued learning."

Developed by Roger Laidig for his book, "Finding Purpose and Joy...
It's a Journey
April, 2014

Exhibit B

PRACTICAL CHRISTIANITY
"Finding Purpose and Joy"
VERSE PACK

1   THE WORD IN MY HEART
Psalm 119:11 I have hidden your word in my heart that I might not sin against you.

2   SEEK FIRST HIS KINGDOM
Matt. 6:33 But seek first his kingdom and his righteousness, and all these things will be given to you as well.

3   LISTEN
James 1:19 My dear brothers, take note of this: Everyone should be quick to listen, slow to speak and slow to become angry,

4   FRUIT
Gal 5:22-23 But the fruit of the Spirit is love, joy, peace, patience, kindness, goodness, faithfulness, gentleness and self-control. Against such things there is no law.

5   LOVE IS …
I Cor 13: 4-5 Love is patient, love is kind. It does not envy, it does not boast, it is not proud. It is not rude, it is not self-seeking, it is not easily angered, it keeps no record of wrongs.

6   THE LAW OF THE HARVEST
Gal 6: 7-8 Do not be deceived: God cannot be mocked. A man reaps what he sows. The one who sows to please his sinful nature, from that

nature will reap destruction; the one who sows to please the Spirit, from the Spirit will reap eternal life.

7   LOVE YOUR ENEMIES
Matt. 5:43-44 "You have heard that it was said, 'Love your neighbor and hate your enemy.' But I tell you: Love your enemies and pray for those who persecute you."

8   THE TWO GREATEST COMMANDMENTS
Matt 22: 37-40 Jesus replied: "'Love the Lord your God with all your heart and with all your soul and with all your mind.' This is the first and greatest commandment. And the second is like it: 'Love your neighbor as yourself.' All the Law and the Prophets hang on these two commandments."

9   LOVE EACH OTHER
John 15:17 This is my command: Love each other.

10   FORGIVE
Matt. 6: 14-15 For if you forgive men when they sin against you, your heavenly Father will also forgive you. But if you do not forgive men their sins, your Father will not forgive your sins.

11   PEACE
Rom 12: 18 If it is possible, as far as it depends on you, live at peace with everyone.

12   UNITY
Eph 4:2-3 Be completely humble and gentle; be patient, bearing with one another in love. Make every effort to keep the unity of the Spirit through the bond of peace.

13   DO NOT BE ANXIOUS

Phil. 4:6-7 Do not be anxious about anything, but in everything, by prayer and petition, with thanksgiving, present your requests to God. And the peace of God, which transcends all understanding, will guard your hearts and your minds in Christ Jesus.

14   ANXIETY

I Peter 5:7 Cast all your anxiety on him because he cares for you.

15   WORRY NOT

Matt 6:31 So do not worry, saying, 'What shall we eat?' or 'What shall we drink?' or 'What shall we wear?'

16   DO NOT WORRY

Matt 6:34 Therefore do not worry about tomorrow, for tomorrow will worry about itself. Each day has enough trouble of its own.

17   DO NOT JUDGE

Luke 6:37 Do not judge, and you will not be judged. Do not condemn, and you will not be condemned. Forgive, and you will be forgiven.

18   ANGER

Eph 4: 31-32 Get rid of all bitterness, rage and anger, brawling and slander, along with every form of malice. Be kind and compassionate to one another, forgiving each other, just as in Christ God forgave you.

19   MONEY

1 Tim 6:10 For the love of money is a root of all kinds of evil. Some people, eager for money, have wandered from the faith and pierced themselves with many griefs.

20   TREASURES

Matt 6: 19 Do not store up for yourselves treasures on earth, where moth and rust destroy, and where thieves break in and steal.

21   TWO MASTERS

Matt 6:24 No one can serve two masters. Either he will hate the one and love the other, or he will be devoted to the one and despise the other. You cannot serve both God and Money.

22   SELFISH AMBITION

Philippians 2: 3 Do nothing out of selfish ambition or vain conceit, but in humility consider others better than yourselves.

23   CHRIST THE CENTER

Psalms 18: 2 The LORD is my rock, my fortress and my deliverer; my God is my rock, in whom I take refuge. He is my shield and the horn of my salvation, my stronghold.

24   THE WAY

John 14:6 Jesus answered, "I am the way and the truth and the life. No one comes to the Father except through me."

25   THE GREAT COMMISSION

Matt 28: 19, 20 Therefore go and make disciples of all nations, baptizing them in the name of the Father and of the Son and of the Holy Spirit, and teaching them to obey everything I have commanded you. And surely I am with you always, to the very end of the age."

Roger Laidig

26   HUSBANDS AND WIVES
Eph 5: 24-25 Now as the church submits to Christ, so also wives should submit to their husbands in everything. Husbands, love your wives, just as Christ loved the church and gave himself up for her

27   FATHERS
Eph 6: 4 Fathers, do not exasperate your children; instead, bring them up in the training and instruction of the Lord.

28   WORK DILIGENTLY
Prov 13: 4 The sluggard craves and gets nothing, but the desires of the diligent are fully satisfied.

29   YOUR BODY
1 Cor 6: 19-20 Do you not know that your body is a temple of the Holy Spirit, who is in you, whom you have received from God? You are not your own; you were bought at a price. Therefore honor God with your body.

30   ATTITUDE
Phil 2: 5 "Your attitude should be the same as that of Christ Jesus"

31   TRUST IN THE LORD
Prov 3: 5-6 Trust in the LORD with all your heart and lean not on your own understanding; in all your ways acknowledge him, and he will make your paths straight.

32   GOD'S CLOTHING
Col 3:12-14 Therefore, as God's chosen people, holy and dearly loved, clothe yourselves with compassion, kindness, humility, gentleness and patience. Bear with each other and forgive whatever grievances you may have against one another. Forgive as the Lord forgave you.

Finding Purpose and Joy

Exhibit C

Suggested Books and Videos

While these books and videos may stretch you a bit, I have recommended them because I have found them to be extremely thought provoking.
There are many other excellent books and videos by these and other authors. This is just a sampling.

BOOKS
- The DNA of Relationships by Gary Smalley

- The Grace Awakening by Charles Swindoll

- The 7 Habits of Highly Effective People by Stephen Covey

- The SPEED of Trust by Stephen M R Covey

- Don't Sweat the Small Stuff and It's All Small Stuff by Richard Carlson

- Falling Upward: A Spirituality for the Two Halves of Life by Richard Rohr

- The Heart of a Leader: Insights on the Art of Influence by Ken Blanchard

- Who Moved My Cheese?: An Amazing Way to Deal with Change in Your Work and in Your Life by Spencer Johnson and Ken Blanchard

- The 15 Invaluable Laws of Growth: Live Them and Reach Your Potential by John C. Maxwell

- LEAD . . . for God'Sake!: A Parable for Finding the Heart of Leadership by Todd Gongwer

VIDEOS

- How Great is our God by Louie Giglio

- Indescribable by Louie Giglio

- The most inspirational videos you will ever see - search the internet for clips about Nick Vujicic

CPSIA information can be obtained at www.ICGtesting.com
Printed in the USA
LVOW13s0024030614

388338LV00001B/163/P

9 781312 127449